To Bee or Not to Bee

John Penberthy

Illustrated by
Laurie Barrows

STERLING

New York / London
www.sterlingpublishing.com

To Bee or Not To Bee makes an endearing gift. Visit the author's website (www.ToBeeBook.com) for information on autographed or personally inscribed copies.

STERLING and the distinctive Sterling logo are registered trademarks of Sterling Publishing Co., Inc.

Library of Congress Cataloging-in-Publication Data

Penberthy, John.
  To bee or not to bee : a book for beeings who feel there's more to life than just making honey / John Penberthy ; illustrated by Laurie Barrows.
      p. cm.
Originally published: Denver, Colo. : Sound Pub., c1987.
ISBN-13: 978-1-4027-4765-6
ISBN-10: 1-4027-4765-9
1. Life--Miscellanea. I. Barrows, Laurie. II. Title.

BD431.P36 2007
128--dc22
                                    2007027398
10 9 8 7 6 5 4 3 2 1

Published by Sterling Publishing Co., Inc.
387 Park Avenue South, New York, NY 10016
© 2007 by Sterling Publishing Co., Inc.
Previously published by Panorama Press, Inc.,
P.O. Box 183, Boulder, CO 80306-0183
Story © 2006 by John Penberthy
Illustrations © 2006 by Laurie Barrows
Distributed in Canada by Sterling Publishing
c/o Canadian Manda Group, 165 Dufferin Street
Toronto, Ontario, Canada M6K 3H6
Distributed in the United Kingdom by GMC Distribution Services
Castle Place, 166 High Street, Lewes, East Sussex, England BN7 1XU
Distributed in Australia by Capricorn Link (Australia) Pty. Ltd.
P.O. Box 704, Windsor, NSW 2756, Australia

Book design and layout by Lise Andersson

Manufactured in the United States of America
All rights reserved

Sterling ISBN-13: 978-1-4027-4765-6
        ISBN-10: 1-4027-4765-9

For information about custom editions, special sales, premium and corporate purchases, please contact Sterling Special Sales Department at 800-805-5489 or specialsales@sterlingpublishing.com.

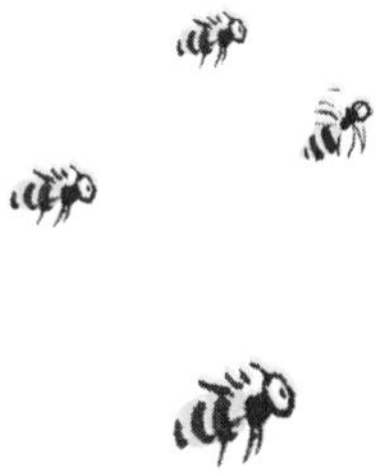

FOREWORD

Bees and I go way back. At the age of one I was sitting in my high chair on our screened porch lost in the innocent oblivion of infancy when a sharp pain suddenly pierced my right forearm. The most traumatic experience of my short life (other than birth), it produced a gusher of tears and wails that brought my mother running. She immediately swatted the bee (its barbed stinger still in my arm), brushed it off, dabbed the sting with ammonia, and smothered me with emotional comfort.

The pain eventually abated. But those ten minutes catapulted me into the realm of conscious awareness and formed my first memory. Funny how pain—physical or emotional—is so good at grabbing our attention, no matter what our age.

Who was to know that event would be auspicious? For the next four decades I had no extraordinary contact with bees, other than high school biology, the occasional bee sting, or sighting of a beehive. Yet one morning I was meditating when a story about bees flashed into my mind and another *apoidea* interjected himself into my awareness, this time more pleasantly. I'm not a person who gets mystical inspirations on any kind of regular basis, but there Buzz Bee was, saying, "The story you've just received is supposed to be a book—write." "Received?" *Downloaded* would have been a better word. The whole thing had flashed into my mind in a nanosecond.

Illustrated, and peppered with wit, humor, and some provocative aphorisms, *To Bee or Not to Bee* is the story of Buzz's search for God. What he ends up finding is himself. Hmmm. It's a journey, that with the help of a newfound friend, confronts him with some of life's most important lessons. He's pulled through them, dragging and kicking, often before he thinks he's ready. But through it all he finds himself expanding and deepening, and knowing that at some level it's all unfolding exactly as it should. Finally, almost in spite of himself, Buzz finds a new acceptance of, and appreciation for, the craziness of life in his honeybee colony.

Sound familiar? If so, maybe, in a way, it's your story too. I hope you enjoy reading *To Bee or Not to Bee* as much as I did writing it.

John Penberthy
Boulder, Colorado

1

IT WAS JUST THE KIND OF DAY Buzz Bee loved most—warm in the sunlight and cool in the shadows. The earth was still damp from the previous afternoon's thunderstorm, and the clover was exquisitely succulent. Dandelion yellow speckled the lush green meadow in every direction, with poppy orange thrown in for good measure. The colors contrasted with the deep blue sky in a way that pleased Buzz beyond words.

The air hummed with the sound of honeybees—bees scouring the meadow for just the right blossom, dipping into flowers for their nectar and pollen, and returning to the hive laden with their nutritious bounty. It was a very industrious scene, Buzz thought, if you stopped to think about it.

As he observed the activity around him, Buzz's mind drifted off into that secret, otherworldly place it loved to explore. Although his eyes were open, the scene before him gradually faded from Buzz's awareness. *Why did anything exist?...Where did it come from?...Why was he here?...What was the point of it all?...Who was he, really?*

A passing worker jolted him back to the task at hand. "Let's go, Buzz, there's work to do."

Embarrassed, Buzz lifted off, landed on a nearby dandelion, and instinctively began probing for nectar. But as he did, he thought, *Here we go again. What's the big rush? This is an incredibly beautiful and abundant valley, yet no one seems at all interested in anything except working to expand the colony.* It already contained far more bees than anyone could count. Buzz didn't see why it was so important for the colony to keep on growing.

When he could hold no more nectar, Buzz moved to another flower and began collecting pollen. Grain by grain he pulled it from the stamen, wadded it into a tight yellow ball, and carefully fastened it to the stiff hairs on the back of his right rear leg. When the ball was secure, he meticulously formed another wad, attaching it to his left rear leg. As he lifted off for the hive, Buzz flew extra hard to compensate for his heavy load.

He landed at the entrance and made his way toward the honeycomb. As always, the passageways were a chaotic maze of bees moving every which way, constantly bumping into one another. And the darkness, heat, and humidity didn't help matters any. It was a miracle that anyone was able to get anywhere. *Surely there must bee a better way*, Buzz thought, as he jostled through the throng.

Apparently he wasn't moving fast enough, for he heard a comment from behind him: "Move it, Buzz, you're holding us all up!"

Then, in his hurry to get to the honeycomb, he bumped into another bee and spilled his pollen. "If you can't do something right, don't do it at all," growled a voice.

Embarrassed, Buzz collected the spilled pollen and hurried to
the honeycomb. He regurgitated his nectar into a honey cell,
as other workers removed his pollen wads and deposited them
into a pollen cell, tamping them down tightly. Not a second was
wasted. Buzz always felt tense inside the hive, but for some
reason today was especially intolerable. He couldn't wait to get
back outside and tried to rush to the entrance, but it was useless

fighting the confusion. It seemed an eternity before he finally saw the welcome slit of daylight piercing the darkness.

Buzz took off and landed on an aspen twig to regain his composure. Was there something wrong with him? Why couldn't he just bee content working all the time like the other bees? But then again, why couldn't they understand that there was more to life than building the hive and raising the brood?

Buzz knew he was as good a worker as any in the colony. Yet today something was really bugging him, and it was beginning to affect his performance. He was already getting a reputation as an eccentric, what with his weird questions and all. Now he was starting to look lazy and incompetent as well.

He surveyed the meadow, the valley, and the mountains beyond. Yes, he knew this was the only meadow in the valley, and a small one at that. He knew that the colony was totally dependent on the clover and flowers that grew there. And he knew that they were in continual competition with the bumblebees, hummingbirds, and butterflies for its limited supply. If he'd heard it once, he'd heard the queen say it a thousand times: "Workers, we have only a small meadow to support us, so let's work extra hard today and get that honeycomb topped off." But then as soon as one honeycomb was filled, they would start working on another. It was endless.

Although he was getting tired of the constant hustle-bustle day after day, it was the subtle fear Buzz sensed throughout the colony that troubled him the most. It was an unspoken, yet driving force that seemed to rob the workers of life. This was an abundant valley, but the bees lived as though starvation were imminent. Something inside told Buzz there was no need to worry; that they would bee provided for, just like the ants and the caterpillars. Why couldn't they just slow their pace, have fewer mouths to feed, and let everyone relax and enjoy life a little more?

And another thing. Why did everyone have to pretend to bee so "up" all the time? The truth was that, while Buzz sometimes felt happy, he also had periods of feeling down and sad. By the tension in the colony, Buzz sensed that he wasn't the only one who felt this way. Yet no one ever said a word about it; it just wasn't acceptable. So he never let it out. This made him feel so phony, which only seemed to make his loneliness and melancholy worse.

Buzz gazed up at the jagged peaks ringing the head of the valley. What was it like up there? And what was beyond? Rumor had it, the land beyond was inhospitable to bees. Some said it was covered with glaciers as far as the eye could see. Others said it dropped off precipitously to an arid desert. Still others said the mountains descended to a vast ocean. One thing was for sure—no one had ever tried to fly over. It was something that bees just didn't do. Buzz himself had flown far enough up-valley to know that once you got above tree line you were at the mercy of the cold, harsh winds that always seemed to be blowing. Still, he couldn't help wondering.

A drone whizzed by: "Buzz, get your rear in gear." It seemed that every time he began to enjoy himself, someone came along and spoiled it. Buzz headed for the meadow, loaded up again, and returned to the hive. The responsible part of him knew he had to do his share, and he felt a bit guilty about his behavior today. He was, after all, a worker bee, and workers are made to work— to build the hive, feed the larvae, keep house, forage, store honey

and pollen, and defend the colony against attack. This latter task was particularly repugnant to Buzz. He hoped he would never bee called upon to fight.

All afternoon Buzz forced himself to do the task at hand and tried not to think about all the things that plagued his curious mind. He was, after all, only a bee. He wasn't going to solve the problems of the world alone. He lived in an industrious society where it was very important to fit in. Already some bees were avoiding him, and he didn't want to bee a complete outcast. From now on, he would muster up some self-discipline and really apply himself. It would bee fine; after all, none of the other bees was complaining.

2

BUZZ spent the next several days working harder than ever. No one could dare accuse him of beeing lazy now. Back and forth, back and forth he flew from hive to clover, always returning with a full load. He hoped that work would distract his mind. He had heard the elders say, "An idle mind is the devil's workshop," and he was beginning to believe it. All his thinking ever got him was trouble. He reminded himself that what he really wanted was to fit in.

At times Buzz was almost able to believe this. He would make two or three mechanical round trips without thinking beyond his required duties. There was a sort of numbness that went along with it, and Buzz tried to convince himself that it was OK.

Yet the truth of the matter was that, for the most part, he continued to think, to question, to bee curious. He just couldn't help it. Foraging was an instinctive activity that required little of his mind. Now he could both work and question it at the same time. It was starting to drive him crazy.

One morning before beginning the day's activities, several bees sitting on a twig close to the hive were observing ants swarming over the anthill below. A few of the ants were dragging a dead fly toward the nest, others were digging, but most just seemed to bee scurrying about aimlessly.

"Look at those mindless ants," jeered one bee.

"Yeah, all they do is run around in circles all day," added another. "The only thing they care about is building a bigger nest and producing more ants. They're like little machines; they have no awareness of themselves, of life. It all seems so pointless."

Buzz could hardly believe his ears—these were the same thoughts he had been having about his own colony! He couldn't contain himself: "But what makes the ants any different from us?"

"Different from us?" retorted the first bee. "Why, everything! For starters, we're a lot bigger."

"But size doesn't mean anything," responded Buzz. "It's all relative."

"Maybe, but they all look alike; you can't tell one from another."

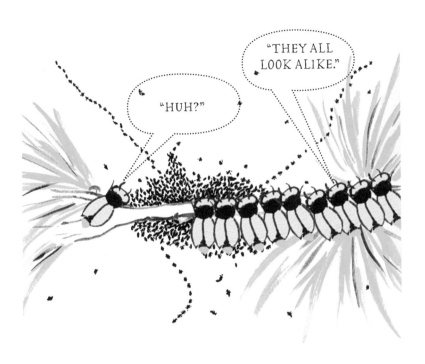

"Plus, we can fly," added the second bee.

"But still," protested Buzz, "we're all living creatures just experiencing life in our own ways."

"You miss the point, Buzz," a third bee added patiently. "Bees are special—we're a much higher form of life than ants. Look at the complexity of our hive, the intricacy of our social structure, the marvel of our reproductive capacities, the way we store honey. Why, ants can't even make honey; they can't begin to compare with us in these areas."

"But I'll bet ants also know a lot that we don't," Buzz shot back. "None of us has ever seen the inside of an ant nest. They seem to do a pretty good job of feeding and reproducing themselves. In fact, I wouldn't bee surprised if their colony is larger than ours."

Buzz could see he was getting himself into hot water. Although a few bees flew off, most stayed, mumbling and exchanging glances of dismay, waiting for the leaders to settle this question once and for all. Finally, one authoritative voice spoke up.

"Quiet, quiet. QUIET! The real difference between us and them still hasn't been addressed. Each of those ants represents only a small piece of his colony; they have little sense of themselves beyond that. We are individuals, aware of ourselves and our surroundings. We have free will to do whatever we please."

Buzz had heard enough. "FREE WILL?" he retorted. "How can you say we have free will when all we do, day after day, is build the nest, forage, and tend the brood?"

"Because, young bee, we have the freedom to choose what part of the nest we work on, which flower to draw nectar from, the route we take to fly there and back, and which larvae to feed. What more freedom could a bee want?"

By now a fairly large crowd was assembled, rumbling in agreement.

Buzz could see he was getting nowhere; he might as well have been arguing with the sky. And whatever goodwill he had generated for himself these last few days was quickly beeing used up. Realizing it was hopeless, he shook his head and, without saying another word, lifted off and headed deep into the forest. There was agreement among the gathered crowd that the truth had been successfully defended.

Buzz flew aimlessly through the woods, totally dejected. It had happened again. It wasn't intentional, but before he knew it he seemed to bee making a fool of himself, becoming further isolated from the rest of the colony. *What is wrong with me? Why can't I fit in?* He landed on the sand along the edge of a stream and stared blankly into the water swirling by.

After a few minutes, Buzz became aware of another presence. He lifted his head and looked a few yards upstream. An older bee with only one cockeyed antenna was sitting eyes-closed in perfect stillness. At that moment the older bee opened his eyes, smiled, and nodded at Buzz. Buzz nodded back.

"Don't let 'em get you down, young fella," the older bee said compassionately.

Buzz was confused. This bee had obviously been here when Buzz arrived. How could he have known about what had just happened in the meadow? "Don't let who get me down?" Buzz asked, feigning ignorance.

"The others," came the casual reply. "Everybody in the colony knows about you by now."

Buzz winced.

The old-timer lifted off and landed next to Buzz. "Name's Bert," he offered.

"Nice to meet you," Buzz replied dejectedly. "I'm Buzz." He looked up and studied this unusual bee. "What are you doing here?" Buzz asked.

"Well...I come here every day to get in touch."

"Get in touch with what?"

"With myself," Bert replied. "It's pretty easy to lose track of that out in the meadow."

Bert suddenly had Buzz's full attention. He had never heard this kind of talk before. "Why did you have your eyes closed?" Buzz asked.

"It helps keep out the distractions."

"Hmmm," Buzz replied thoughtfully. Something told him it was safe to speak his mind with Bert, and he felt his defenses softening.

Bert smiled at Buzz reassuringly. "I've had my eye on you, Buzz. You remind me of myself when I was younger. You're different, and you'll have to come to terms with that if you're going to become whoever it is you're meant to bee. I know beeing different can bee difficult at times, but there can also bee... incredible richness."

Buzz was comforted by the knowledge that he wasn't the only

bee in the colony to have such strange inclinations. Yet he didn't see much hope in Bert's advice. "But every time I open my mouth, I seem to put my foot into it. If I speak my mind, I'm an outcast. If I stifle myself, I'm miserable."

"You've got to find middle ground, son," Bert responded. "Look, you're a worker and you've got to do your share if you're going to live in this colony. Yet that doesn't mean you can't bee who you really are. It's not work that's keeping you from beeing content; it's your attitude—thinking that work is separate from your personal life, that work is the sole point of life. You can work and think at the same time; I've seen you. You can work and appreciate the beauty of this valley at the same time. And you can certainly mix a little relaxation and exploration into your daily routine. It's all a state of mind. Bee in the world; not of it."

"But what about all the other bees who are wasting their lives working, working, working, day after day, till they drop dead?"

"Don't bee so concerned about them, Buzz. They're doing what feels right to them, just as you are. Try to bee more understanding. The power of the mind lies in perceiving differences; the power of the heart lies in perceiving similarities. Which power are you using?"

"I just see what I see," Buzz resisted.

"Another thing—don't bee so worried about what they think of you," suggested Bert. "They've got different priorities, and if you spend your life trying to please them, you'll bee miserable. Just do your part and let your life, not your words, influence them. Life is a journey from I to we."

Bert's kindly, soft-spoken manner impressed Buzz deeply, and he was already starting to feel better. Maybe there was hope after all.

3

THE NEXT MORNING before heading off to the meadow, Buzz overheard a group of bees participating in their morning devotions. He had never felt much of an attraction to religion, but this morning for some reason he was drawn to the group. He positioned himself nearby and listened. The leader was just finishing a prayer: "...and finally, Lord, we ask that all those in the colony who have not yet accepted your word bee shown the way so that they too may bee saved. Amen."

Saved? Buzz thought. *Maybe this is what I've been looking for.* He mingled with the crowd, listening to the conversation, trying to get more information without drawing attention to himself. He overheard someone say, "It just goes to show you, the love of honey is the root of all evil." Buzz thought this sounded a bit odd, given that the bee who said it was one of the most honey-hungry bees in the colony.

The leader, Bobby, had had his eye on Buzz for weeks. He well understood what Buzz had been going through. He had seen it a hundred times and felt a sense of compassion for the confused young bee. Certain that he knew the exact solution to Buzz's problems, he became excited at the prospect of saving another soul. Bobby gradually made his way through the crowd toward Buzz and, with a sincere tone of concern, asked, "What brings you here today, son?"

"I'm not exactly sure," Buzz replied tentatively.

"Well, we welcome you; you've come to the right place. I know you've been a bit distraught lately, and, you know, if you just turn your life over to the Lord, you too can bee saved."

"Saved from what?" Buzz asked.

"Why, from hell, from eternal damnation when you die."

"But why would I go to hell?"

"Because you're a sinner, just like the rest of us. And if you don't live a pious life and ask the Supreme Beeing for forgiveness, you don't stand a chance of going to heaven."

The notion that he was a sinner was news to Buzz. He had always considered himself to bee quite moral. Maybe he wasn't perfect, but he never did anything to intentionally hurt anyone. But then again, maybe the Supreme Beeing took a different view of things. Bobby certainly seemed to know. Buzz wanted to hear more about the consequences of beeing a sinner. "What's hell like?" he asked.

Squinting, Bobby's face took on a fierce quality, and he spoke in a foreboding voice. "Hell is the realm of Beelzebub, the Devil. It's like an eternal forest fire, with no escape and no relief, ever. Although the pain is unbearable, you never die; you just suffer in misery with all the other damned bees, crying and moaning in agony forever."

Something didn't feel right, but Buzz wanted to hear more. "What's heaven like?"

Bobby instantly relaxed. A rapt expression overcame his face as he looked skyward. "Heaven is the realm of the Supreme Beeing. It's an infinite, lush meadow filled with tasty wildflowers of every description. There's no need to work, and there's never any discord. There are no bears, and the weather's always perfect. All the bees' needs are provided for, and everyone is happy all the time."

It actually sounded a bit boring to Buzz. "Can ants go to heaven?"

"No, only bees," Bobby replied authoritatively.

"But we don't go there till we die?"

"Right, if you're good and believe in the Supreme Beeing."

"But what about *this* life, the one we're living right now?"

"This life is simply preparation, a test for the hereafter."

It was all beginning to sound a bit contrived. If Buzz were going to believe all this, he would want to see some benefits in this life, not on the chance that he'd bee rewarded *if* there were a hereafter. "What's the Supreme Beeing like?"

"The Supreme Beeing is spirit that is everywhere and all-powerful. He created us in his likeness, which means that he thinks and acts like a bee. This is how we know his wishes. He loves us and watches over us."

Buzz considered Bobby's words carefully. "But if God is everywhere and all-powerful, then where does the Devil exist?"

Bobby felt a little frustrated by Buzz's simple logic but tried not to bee condescending. "The Devil is a crafty fellow, always tempting us with evil, and when we give in he gets a foothold."

"So the Devil really exists in our minds?"

"No, no!" Bobby replied curtly. "The Devil is an evil spiritual beeing that exists in hell."

"So God exists everywhere except where the Devil is?" Buzz reasoned innocently.

"I suppose you could say that," Bobby replied uncertainly and increasingly exasperated.

"But that would mean that God really isn't everywhere and all-powerful."

Bobby felt his patience slipping further and strained to maintain his smile as he replied as kindly as possible. "Buzz, this religion can't bee figured out; it must simply bee accepted on faith."

Buzz silently pondered all this for a few moments, trying to make sense of it. But he was having a hard time believing something that wasn't logical. He wondered why God would give us reason and logic if he didn't want us to use it. "How do you know all this?" he asked.

"It is knowledge that has been passed down for hundreds of generations," Bobby replied.

Buzz wondered why bees from hundreds of generations ago

would know any more than bees today. If anything, he thought it should bee the other way around. But he kept these thoughts to himself. "And you say God loves all of us?"

"Absolutely," Bobby replied earnestly, feeling he was finally beginning to get through to Buzz.

"But if God loves all of us, why would he send some of us to hell?" It was an honest question, but Buzz had gone one step too far.

"Because some of us are remorseless sinners and must bee punished!" Bobby replied tensely. "You ask too many questions, young bee, and if you don't change, it's going to lead you to a heap of trouble come Judgment Day."

Buzz didn't want to start another argument and was about to take off when another bee who had been listening to the conversation spoke up. "I know this all must sound a bit confusing to you at first, son, but it starts to fit together after a while. It really all boils down to brotherly love."

Buzz was aghast. Wasn't this the same bee that had been cracking wasp jokes only a week earlier? He had heard enough. As he lifted his wings to take off, Bobby invited Buzz to devotions that night. Buzz thanked him, said he needed time to think it all over, and took off for the meadow.

4

BUZZ was more confused than ever. All his life he had felt an intuitive knowing of God—a sort of oneness with nature—and that there was no need to formalize it. Yet now that he felt a greater yearning, what he was hearing just didn't fit at all. Although he tried to distract himself with work, it just made things worse. He finally broke away from his routine to find Bert.

"I've always had a problem with the word *God*," Bert offered after Buzz finished rambling through his confusion. "It means too many different things to different bees. To most folks, God is some giant, vindictive spirit-bee in the sky, and I just don't buy that."

"Well, what do you think God is?" Buzz asked.

"I don't know," Bert replied. "I don't think we can comprehend God, because we can only perceive things through our limited bee perspective and God is so much greater than that. As best I can tell, God seems to bee the Universal Creative Force...the Laws of Nature...the Way of Things...What Is. I think that's about the best we can come up with. Beyond that, we just have to live in the mystery."

This made sense to Buzz, but the thought of holding beliefs so different from the rest of the colony intimidated him, and he said so to Bert.

"Religion doesn't come from God; it comes from bees," offered Bert. "Most folks don't think they can find God on their own, so they rely on others to show them the way. Problem is, God is within as much as anywhere else, and most bees have a hard time believing they're divine. So they look outside themselves in religion or ritual to try to satisfy their longing for God."

"Is that why they feel the need to worship God?" Buzz asked.

"Yep, it's supposed to bee a way of showing appreciation," Bert replied. "But to me, God is so far beyond needing appreciation from us insignificant little bees, it seems kind of silly. I think a lot of folks worship more with the idea of keeping on God's good side than beeing thankful for their existence. Plus, unless you're careful, a lot can get lost in the routine and rituals."

"RELIGION DOESN'T COME FROM GOD, IT COMES FROM BEES."

"I know what you mean, Bert," Buzz said. "The times when I feel the greatest sense of oneness with things are when I intentionally stop and really feel the awe of our existence in this beautiful valley. It's like the genuine experience of appreciation alone is enough; it doesn't have to bee directed at anyone."

"Well, if God is within..." Bert's voice trailed off.

A long, warm silence ensued as Buzz and Bert stood there, absorbing the meaning of what had just been said. Buzz felt a deep sense of gratitude toward Bert. Although he hadn't spent that much time with him, he felt as if he had known the old fellow his whole life. He thought back to the day they first met. "Bert, can I ask you a personal question?"

"Sure," Bert replied. "Anything."

"Remember when we first met and you were sitting there with your eyes closed?"

"Yep."

"What were you praying about?" Buzz asked.

"I wasn't praying, I was just sitting."

"Well, why did you have your eyes closed?" Buzz inquired. "What were you thinking about?"

"Actually I was trying not to think," responded Bert. "I was focusing on my breathing."

"Why?"

"Well, as I said before, to keep out the distractions, so I can get in touch with myself. Focusing on my breathing helps to deepen me and let more of who I really am come out."

"Do you pray?" Buzz asked.

"Not much any more," said Bert. "To me, praying is usually asking for something, trying to get life to bend to our wishes. My sitting is more about calming down and listening, about gaining control of my own mind. I've found that I have much better results controlling my own mind—which ultimately determines my experience—than trying to control everything else."

This made so much sense to Buzz. He could not believe his good fortune in encountering this wise old bee. For the first time he felt validated and supported for his unorthodox ways of viewing the world. "Bert, I can't tell you how much I appreciate your help," Buzz said. "It means so much to me to know that I'm not the only one in the colony that's so different."

"It truly is my pleasure, Buzz," said Bert in a fatherly way. "But you've got to bee careful about relying too much on me or anyone else. Each bee must find his own truth. Hopefully you've learned by now there's no sense in looking to the rest of the colony for your well-beeing because they don't have it to give to you in the first place. The only place you're going to find it is within. I can bee a guide, but that's all. Don't believe anything anyone tells you—and that includes me—unless it rings true inside."

Buzz thought about how nice that sounded, but when he recalled his experience of looking within, a sense of sadness arose. "Bert, to bee perfectly honest, I really haven't had much luck looking within. It seems the more I look within, the more miserable I become."

"Nobody ever promised that becoming who you really are would bee easy," Bert replied. "It hasn't always been that way for me."

Buzz kicked loose a grain of pollen that had stuck to his leg and gazed out over the meadow, feeling himself sinking. "I guess I'm afraid I'll bee a failure."

"Who's to say what's failure and what's success? Either way, you've grown. Success is simply beeing on your path. Only through experience can we expand beyond our limited bee perspective and start to see the larger picture of things."

"What's that?"

Bert looked at Buzz thoughtfully. "Let's save it for another time. You've already got more than enough to chew on."

"Oh, come on, Bert!" Buzz protested. He wasn't about to let Bert bring him this far and then leave him hanging. "I've been able to handle everything you've told me so far. It's going to come out sooner or later. Come on!"

"Well...all right," Bert relented, and then collected his thoughts. "I've only glimpsed it a few times, but I can tell you that once you've experienced the divine perspective, you know once and for all that everything is perfect—that this Universe, this Earth, this Valley, this Life are without flaw."

"Perfect? Without flaw?" Buzz felt his defenses coming on. "How can you say everything is perfect when there is so much prejudice and hostility and sickness and death in this valley? When I'm so unhappy lately? Are you saying all this is perfect?"

"From an expanded perspective, yes. These things are just opportunities to learn the lessons necessary for us to realize our own perfection."

A long, uneasy silence ensued as Buzz blankly gazed out over the meadow. Bert finally spoke. "Let me ask you a question. Do you believe God is everywhere?"

"Well, yes, of course."

"Do you believe God is perfect?"

"Yes."

"Then...by definition...everything is perfect," Bert concluded. He peered at the distant peaks with a faraway look in his eyes. "Don't you see, Buzz? Perfection isn't some state of affairs, it's a state of mind."

"Hmmm." At some level, Bert's words felt right to Buzz, but he was struggling to comprehend them intellectually. "You mean even unhappiness is perfect?"

"Yep, because it causes us to look deeper. Any time I'm unhappy or angry or whatever, I try to see it as feedback that my consciousness is out of sync with The Way. To me, that's hell. It's not always easy and it takes discipline, but I know from my own experience that, with enough practice, a bee can achieve fulfillment and contentment beyond understanding."

"Fulfillment? Contentment? I want to bee happy and..."

"Never sad," Bert interrupted.

"Well, yes. What's wrong with that?"

"I suppose you also want up without down, soft without hard, cold without hot, and good without bad?"

Buzz was caught off guard; his mind was reeling. Bert was right—this was a lot to absorb. Both bees went silent, staring into the distance.

Sensing Buzz's confusion, Bert finally spoke up. "Don't you see, Buzz? Everything is relative; the instant you define one condition, you've created its opposite. How can you have cold unless you know what hot is? How can you have up without down? Happy without sad?"

"But Bert, you seem to bee happy most of the time."

"Buzz, most of what you see in me isn't happiness as much as it is peace—the inner peace that comes from accepting this valley just the way it is. Whatever happiness I experience is incidental. Happiness cannot bee pursued; it must ensue."

SPLAT! A large drop of rain hit the ground not a foot away. They looked up to see that the intensity of their conversation had distracted them from a thunderstorm building above. The sky had grown dark, and a cool wind was kicking up. One of the cardinal rules of beeing was *Don't get caught in the rain.* A bee with waterlogged wings was totally useless, and a direct hit from a large raindrop, or worse, a hailstone, could bee fatal. Buzz and Bert bolted for the nearest boulder, scrambled underneath, and peered out intently as the storm grew.

Buzz flinched as lightning crashed into the top of a nearby tree. A gust of wind suddenly blasted through, whipping the treetops like blades of grass. The sky was dark and ominous, but uncannily reluctant, yielding only sporadic, large raindrops. The storm seemed to bee toying with them. Buzz had never sensed such tension.

And then suddenly, it let loose. Driven by a roaring wind, curtains of rain raced across the meadow. Lightning crashed all around them, its thunder rattling their small bodies. It lit the meadow in bright, eerie flashes that sent chills down Buzz's spine. He glanced nervously at Bert to see the cold whiteness reflecting an excited smile on the old bee's face. Water trickled in to where they stood, forcing them to higher ground. Buzz tried to relax, but couldn't. As the storm intensified, it occurred to him that the hive might bee in jeopardy. There was no hail, at least not yet, but the wind was so strong that it might rip the hive right off the branch from which it hung. Buzz kept looking in the direction of the hive, but the rain was so dense that it obscured his vision. Finally he caught a glimpse and saw the hive whipping furiously, almost horizontal.

Bert saw it too. "That could bee really serious," he said.

Finally the wind and lightning subsided, and the storm eased into a steady downpour. Still the two bees stood there silently, each absorbed in his own thoughts. When the rain abated to just a sprinkle, Buzz and Bert and every other bee in the valley flew straight to the hive to assess the damage.

"It's hanging on by only a few strands," they heard as they approached. "A few more minutes of that wind and it would

have been gone." Several bees entered and called to those inside to evacuate immediately. Within a minute every bee was out, except for the queen, who was too large to fly.

Everyone sensed the urgency of the situation. Another strong gust, and the hive could go. Instinctively all workers began nibbling on bark, which they chewed into pulp, which they then passed on to other workers, who applied it to the remaining strands to reinforce them. Within a few hours the hive was out of jeopardy, everyone began to breathe easier, and by sunset the repair was largely complete.

5

THE MOOD among the colony that evening was solemn, to say the least. It wasn't until the work had been completed that the reality sank in of how close to catastrophe they had come. Everyone kept repeating, "Just one more gust and..."

Everyone except Bobby, who kept repeating, "This is retribution from God. We must repent and lead more pious lives."

Buzz kept on coming back to what Bert had been saying about perfection. Here they had just about lost their hive, and Bert would probably say that was perfect too. Who was he to make that kind of judgment? Buzz was having a hard time accepting that everything was perfect.

The next morning Buzz found Bert basking on a Black-eyed Susan. "How do you know all this stuff you've been telling me?" he asked.

"I just pay close attention. And I'm very careful about believing what I hear from other bees; I always check it out inside first." Bert stared blankly into the distance, giving Buzz the feeling his mind was somewhere far away. "Don't you see? It's perfect that we think life is imperfect. It's what keeps each of us on our own unique path until eventually we realize our own perfection, our Oneness. In my book, that's heaven."

"IT'S PERFECT THAT WE THINK LIFE IS IMPERFECT."

"But what's the point of it all?'

"I don't know that there is one, beyond moment-to-moment existence. But when I look around I see one factor common to all life, and that is expansion. Every bit of life seems to bee trying to fill a greater niche, to become all it can bee."

"But Bert, this whole expansion mentality is exactly what drives me crazy about this place."

"I'm not just talking about outer expansion. There's already plenty of that going on. I'm talking about that whole other world of inner expansion—what you're going through."

Buzz nodded in thoughtful agreement. "And we do that by looking within and seeking our true identity."

"Right; our basic problem is that we perceive ourselves as separate, apart from others and our surroundings, apart from God. But everything is also interconnected, all One. Separate and One at the same time. Sometimes words and concepts just get in the way."

Buzz slowly contemplated this and finally spoke. "Bert, I can comprehend my oneness in my mind, but I don't *feel* it; I don't experience it."

"Exactly," replied Bert. "That's the big challenge. Not to just understand it, but to *bee* it so that it's your identity."

"So how do I get there?"

Bert thought for a moment and then simply said,
"Hold your breath."

"Hold my breath?" Buzz repeated, not seeing the relevance to
the conversation.

"Right, just hold your breath."

"OK," said Buzz skeptically, as he inhaled deeply. He glanced at
Bert, awaiting the next instruction, but Bert looked away and
began quietly humming. Buzz obediently continued holding his
breath, wondering what this could possibly bee about. After a
minute his face began turning red, while Bert just went on
humming. Buzz held on until he felt he would pass out, then
finally exhaled loudly and gulped several large breaths to regain
his equilibrium.

Just as Buzz opened his mouth to ask Bert the point of all this, Bert looked at him and said, "Still feel separate?"

Gradually a broad smile of comprehension spread across Buzz's face. "I *am* connected with all things," he said slowly. "I can't live for even a few minutes without oxygen. And oxygen comes from plants...which need sunlight...and soil...and rain...and even gravity...and...it just goes on and on."

"Yep. This tendency we have to identify ourselves as separate is an arbitrary choice we make that most of us aren't even aware of. We can just as well identify ourselves with the One, if we bring the necessary intention and mindfulness to it."

Bert looked at Buzz and could see by the furrow in his brow that he was again lost in thought. He burst out laughing, startling Buzz.

"What's so funny?" Buzz asked.

"Buzz, it seems that you believe if you just think about all this hard and long enough you'll figure it out—in your mind."

"Well, yeah, I suppose I do," replied Buzz defensively.

"Thinking is certainly a part of it," said Bert, "but by no means all of it. There's a higher part of you that can control even your mind, but you can only connect with it through observation and experience. The mind is a wonderful servant but a terrible master."

Buzz tried not to think for a while but found it impossible. "Bert," he began, "I know intellectually that oxygen and trees and soil and whatnot are necessary for life, but what I want is to feel that connection with God."

"You're too obsessed with your ideas of God," Bert responded.

"But I thought it was good to bee obsessed with God!" Buzz protested.

"I didn't say you're too obsessed with God," corrected Bert. "I said you're too obsessed with your *ideas* of God."

Once again Buzz felt his confusion building. "But really, Bert, aren't our ideas of God the only way we have of comprehending him?"

"No," said Bert. "They get in the way more often than not. God cannot bee comprehended; only experienced."

Buzz closed his eyes and let go of his thoughts as best he could. "Well, that means God is everything," said Buzz disappointedly.

"Exactly!" Bert replied excitedly. "Including you! Instead of thinking so much, fully experience whatever it is you're doing, as in Living Your Life, moment-to-moment."

Buzz was struggling to comprehend all that had been said. Bert then added, "The greatest present is the present."

At some level Buzz knew what Bert was saying was right, but he was beginning to feel overwhelmed. Bert had given him a lot to absorb and he was about to excuse himself when Bert made yet another point.

"Look Buzz, I don't know how else to say this, but you need to stop thinking of everything in terms of God. It just obscures things. Yes, some unimaginable power created this universe and this planet and this valley and us. But so what? Ultimately we're still here with our lives to lead. You keep injecting your ideas of God into everything, and it just fouls it up—I call it the Divine Detour. It's fine to bee on it for a while, but if you don't eventually get through it, you just keep going around in circles."

Whoa! Buzz thought. Bert was starting to sound pretty radical, if not sacrilegious. For the first time Buzz began to seriously question what Bert was saying.

"And while we're on the subject," Bert continued, "I also encourage you to think deeper about the word *spiritual*. An awful lot of bees get tripped up thinking God is just spiritual. When you do that you forget that God is just as much the physical—bees, trees, soil, sunlight. Why relegate God to only the spiritual realm, when we have all these miraculous physical reminders right in front of us all the time? I prefer to use the word *sacred*."

"Yeah, but you have to admit the physical seems so mundane," Buzz commented.

"That's because you're numb," replied Bert.

Bert could bee pretty blunt at times. But Buzz had to admit that there was a numb quality to his life. Overwhelmed, he breathed a sigh of hopelessness.

Sensing Buzz's dejection, Bert added, "Now, are you ready for the good news?"

"I guess," replied Buzz, feeling a little sorry for himself.

"Knowing that you're numb is a huge first step. Most bees live their entire lives without even acknowledging to themselves that they're numb. And wanting to do something about it is a major second step."

"So I'm two steps into this process," Buzz summarized. "Where do I go from here?"

"Practice paying close attention. Try to see the sacred in everything."

Practice, Buzz thought. *More work and effort.*

"Stick with it, Buzz," said Bert. "Give it time. This is a way of life, not something to bee accomplished in an afternoon. Remember, God isn't some giant spirit bee in the sky or idea in your mind. Everything is divine—you, me, Bobby, this boulder, the meadow—even Boris."

6

A QUARTER MILE AWAY Boris Bear was rambling
through the woods, when an ever-so-slight scent of honey
wafted by his nose. It reminded him once again of the sweet
treasure that was always so close, yet so far away. As a cub he
had learned the hard way that, although bees are small, they
can sure cause a bear a lot of pain. Through sheer determination
he had managed to get a taste of honey then, and had never
forgotten that it was by far the most delectable item on the
forest menu. Boris decided to check out the hive, on the remote
chance that it had been deserted. When it came to honey, no
stone was left unturned.

Buzz was storing a fresh load of pollen when he heard the alert go out. Heart pounding, he made his way through the frantic mob to the entrance of the hive and looked down. His worst fears were confirmed. Five feet below, Boris clung to the tree, trying to climb and swat bees off his face at the same time.

This was a life-or-death situation to the colony, or so everyone had been told. All workers were to automatically attack the intruder without concern for the fact that those who stung him would die. Buzz had been rebuked when he once asked why they couldn't just rebuild the hive in a safer place and avoid all the loss of life. It was a matter of pride, he was told; they just couldn't let Boris push them around. Even though he was a clumsy oaf, he was big, and they had to stand up to him. Buzz also sensed that some of the more macho bees actually wanted Boris to attack so they could taste combat. He couldn't understand why they were so eager to risk death for the sake of pride.

Buzz was pushed off the hive by the mass of bees taking to the air. Below, a swarm of them furiously orbited Boris's head, targeting the exposed parts of his face—lips, nose, eyes, and ears. As soon as one bee stung him, it took off, mortally ripping its barbed stinger from its body, making room for another to attack. Buzz circled around the swarm, observing the carnage, but keeping his distance.

It was decision time for Boris. His face was a mass of bees; he couldn't even open one eye for fear of getting stung in an

eyeball. Growling and groaning, he finally realized that today wasn't his day for honey and he began to retreat. Everyone breathed a sigh of relief except the macho bees, who pursued him deep into the forest.

The hive was a nightmare of wailing and moaning. Hundreds of dead and dying bees lay on the ground beneath the hive. Dozens more mortally wounded bees returned with gaping holes in their rumps to die their slow deaths. Everyone was proud that the hive had been successfully defended, and this gave solace to the dying. As each bee died, his body was dragged to the entrance and pushed over the edge. Over the next day, a huge pile of dead bees accumulated beneath the hive, the smell of death rising to engulf it. It was the most repugnant scene Buzz had ever witnessed, yet in some perverse way it seemed to build camaraderie among the members of the colony.

That evening a passing worker pointed at Buzz and said, "There's the coward." Buzz was shocked—he had been noticed! He tried to ignore it and move on, but one of the macho bees, Buster, blocked his path. "You sure kept your distance from Boris this morning," he sneered.

Buzz felt his stinger throbbing, yet he remained calm. He remembered Bert cautioning him not to rely on others for his sense of well-beeing. Then he heard himself say, "I don't believe in needless war and I refuse to sacrifice my life for the pride of the colony. There are other ways to deal with Boris. If everyone felt the way I do, we wouldn't have that pitiful pile of dead bees down there."

"Boris is evil and must bee stopped," Buster retorted. "We can't just let him dictate how we live."

"But if we gradually rebuild the hive in a safe place out of his reach, we'll never have to deal with him again," Buzz asserted.

"And what do you think that would do for the morale of the colony? We'd bee the laughing stock of the valley."

"Maybe for a while, but it would ultimately make us stronger because we wouldn't lose hundreds of workers every time Boris gets a craving for honey."

"Out of the question. Boris has to know he can't push us around."

Buzz's nerve was building and, on a hunch, he asked Buster a precarious question. "By the way, if you hate Boris so much, why are you here talking to me and not on that death heap down there?"

Buster stuttered, "I...I..." but before he could finish, Buzz was gone.

The next morning Buzz couldn't stop pondering what Bert had said about perfection. The old part of him wanted to dismiss it as total nonsense. How could hundreds of bees dying in a bear raid bee perfect? Yet there was a new part of him that was excited by this notion; something about it rang true to the very core of his beeing.

Buzz found Bert basking in the sun on a dandelion puff. "Tell me how hundreds of bees dying in a bear raid is perfect."

"No, you tell me." Bert sensed that Buzz was getting lazy.

"Hmmm. Well...I suppose first of all that there really is nothing evil about Boris liking honey. It just seems evil from our perspective because it happens to bee our honey he wants. Given all the pain we cause him, he probably thinks we're as evil as we think he is."

"Good. Say more."

"Well...although it seems as if those bees died protecting the hive, their deaths also have another purpose—to prod us to look for better alternatives. The denser we are, the harder the lessons. Those bees didn't have to die. The problem, though, is that most folks are either too lazy or proud or bound by tradition to face up to the need for change. But unless we do, we'll just keep making the same mistakes again and again. The perfection seems to lie in the process, in the opportunity for learning."

"Spoken like a true teacher!" Bert proudly stroked one of Buzz's antennas with his own.

Buzz had never thought of himself as a teacher before.

That faraway look again spread over Bert's face. "Every incident that occurs carries with it potential lessons. Lessons are the flip side of experience. Learning is what got us this far and what will take us wherever we're going. Although most bees see this world as an end unto itself, it's also a prop for learning, a vehicle for greater awareness."

Buzz felt a tingle spread through his body, as this revelation dawned on him. "Bert, why didn't you tell me this before?"

"I've been trying to," Bert deadpanned.

Both bees laughed. All this was so new; the bear raid really had driven the point home. Bert then noticed that familiar serious expression coming over Buzz's face and prepared for another question.

"Bert, can I ask you a personal question?"

"Have I ever turned you down?"

Buzz smiled sheepishly. "How did you lose your antenna?"

"Bear raid," Bert replied. "Just like the one yesterday."

"What happened?"

"Well, it was a long time ago. I was young and full of myself. I'm foraging one day, when suddenly I hear the alarm go out and make a beeline for the hive. There's Boris climbing for it. I'm one of the first to reach him. I land right on his nose and am sticking my stinger in, when he swats and knocks me and a bunch of others right off. I black out for a while, and when I come to I'm lying on the ground surrounded by dead and dying bees. Boris is nowhere to bee seen. I think I'm dying because I'm sure my stinger and my rump are lodged in Boris's nose. But I look down and they're still there. Apparently my stinger wasn't quite far enough in for the barbs to take hold. Anyway, I stand up and my legs are wobbly and both wings are strained and my antenna is missing, but everything works. The way I figure, it was a miracle that I survived, and from that point on, I had a whole new perspective on life; things were never quite the same. Brain damage, probably..."

Buzz chuckled.

"Each of us awakens in our own way and in our own time," Bert added. "Some of us are denser than others. And some of us are just plain lucky."

Buzz pondered this for a while before speaking. "You know, you could say that those bees were my teachers, even though they didn't intend to bee."

"Yep, we can all learn plenty from each other—even those we think don't know as much as we do—if we can just set our egos aside. There's no shortage of lessons. We're all each others' students and teachers."

Buzz just sat there thinking. "You know, this perspective stuff is amazing. Instead of viewing everything from inside out, it's like shifting your consciousness to perceiving things from outside in, moving out beyond our own bodies. It's like we can realize we're much more than just bees."

Bert chuckled knowingly. "Does seem that way, doesn't it?"

Better alternatives. All day those words kept resonating through Buzz's mind as he foraged. On the one hand he could begin to see the perfection of the bear raid; but on the other hand he could see that it was avoidable. He had become obsessed with how vulnerable the hive was. First the thunderstorm, and now Boris. He couldn't believe how unconcerned the rest of the bees were. It was just a matter of time before the worst happened. Buzz had already expressed his concerns and had been rebuked, but there was no reason why he couldn't help the colony bee prepared for the worst, if and when it happened.

The next morning he began scouting new locations to rebuild the hive. Trees were out of the question—too vulnerable. Bushes wouldn't work for the same reason. No, he needed to find a place that was both inaccessible to bears and protected from the weather. Back and forth he flew, eying the landscape for some possible solution, but having no luck. He was up-valley and about to turn back around when suddenly something told him to look up. There, before him, lay the answer. Why hadn't someone thought of this before?

7

AS SPRING DISAPPEARED INTO SUMMER, Buzz spent more and more time with Bert. It was becoming obvious that Bert wasn't going to bee around much longer. The old-timer's body was giving in to the high-energy rigors of beeing. Although his mind was as sharp as ever, he had trouble staying aloft even a minute. And no one needed to say that once a bee can no longer fly, well...

Buzz found himself questioning everything. Occasionally he had glimpses of a new inner knowing, but just as often he felt a growing sense of pain and frustration. He'd have an hour or a day where he felt gloriously alive and at one with the universe

and he'd happily think that he'd finally found what he was looking for. But sooner or later he'd notice that state of mind fading away. Try as he might, there was nothing he could do to recapture it. Then, before he knew it, he was back in his old state of mind, which seemed even worse than before because of what he had just experienced. It often hurt terribly—Buzz didn't know he could feel so bad, so unstable, so confused. It was times like these that he began questioning why he was spending so much time with Bert when all it did was upset him. Bert's "wisdom" sounded good, but was it really for Buzz? Could it lead to any sort of lasting contentment in his life?

Buzz found himself increasingly drawn to the pass. In fact, he could hardly stop thinking about it. One afternoon he flew up to the tree line to take another look. It was definitely treacherous— the pass loomed another 3,000 feet above, strong winds gusted around unpredictably and the thin air made for tough flying. The cold, gray rocks were a formidable contrast to the soft, green meadow. Yet something told Buzz it was do-able.

That evening when Buzz told him about it, Bert seemed to bee a little down on the idea. "No matter where you go, there you are," he quipped. "The only way out is in."

"I suppose, but something tells me I need to find out what's on the other side."

"That's fine. Just don't think it's going to solve your problems."

Buzz was reluctant to admit it, but he knew Bert was right. He was starting to get a little tired of Bert always beeing right.

"Now, tell me about this urge of yours," Bert continued.

"Well, it's hard to describe. It's like I'm obsessed; I can't get it off my mind. It just seems like I've got to try it."

"What's holding you back?"

"What's holding me back? It's dangerous up there! The wind blows like crazy, it's really cold, and it's a long way straight up. I could get killed—that's what's holding me back!"

"To the extent you're afraid to die, you're afraid to live."

"Easy for you to say," Buzz shot back. Bert's triteness was really bugging him. Buzz could never quite figure him out. One minute he seemed against the idea, and the next he seemed for it. "Bert, I know you're trying to help me, but sometimes I get so frustrated by all your double-talk. Why don't you just come right out and tell me what you think I should do?"

Bert sensed the tension in Buzz's voice. "It pains me to see you struggling, Buzz, and sometimes I do want to give you advice, but what's right for me isn't necessarily right for you. My job is to help you find your own answers."

Buzz's frustration was mounting and he began to feel sorry for himself. He wished he could go back and start over and bee just like everyone else.

"TO THE EXTENT YOU'RE AFRAID TO DIE,
YOU'RE AFRAID TO LIVE."

"There's no turning back now; you know too much," Bert interjected.

Buzz looked up suspiciously at the old bee. Was Bert reading his mind? "Things are just changing too fast," Buzz complained. "I can't take this much change."

"All things take place by change," replied Bert.

A long, uncomfortable silence ensued. Buzz felt he was near his breaking point and suddenly had the fervent wish that someone would simply come along and make it all better.

"Each bee is responsible for his own salvation," Bert said the instant Buzz finished his thought.

Buzz looked at him incredulously. "Were you reading my mind?"

Bert changed the subject. "It doesn't all have to bee pain and effort, you know. Life's too important to bee taken so seriously. In life, pain is inescapable. Suffering is optional."

Buzz felt his patience slipping and thought if he heard one more platitude he would explode.

Sensing opportunity, Bert added, " Do nothing and nothing is left undone."

Suddenly a flash of rage surged through Buzz. "What is that supposed to mean?" he snapped. "Why can't you talk straight to me? You've screwed me up for life, and you just keep feeding me more! And what's worse is I keep taking it! I'm sick and tired

of you and all your mystical mumbo-jumbo! None of it makes sense; all it does is make me miserable! I'm getting out of here!"

Buzz was furious. He lifted off and headed for the solace of the forest, but quickly circled back around and whizzed by Bert, screaming, "LEAVE ME ALONE! I CAN'T TAKE ANY MORE!"

Buzz headed deep into the forest to his spot by the stream and fumed the rest of the day. Back and forth, back and forth he paced by the water's edge. His life was falling apart, and his best friend was responsible. What right did that old loony have to brainwash him like this? A part of Buzz secretly wished Bert would die soon. It would sure solve a lot of his problems. Then he could get back to beeing normal again.

The next day, Buzz purposely avoided Bert. He had calmed down, but decided that although the old-timer was well-meaning, he was getting senile and Buzz just didn't need any more of his "wisdom" for a while. Buzz needed to concentrate on regaining his sanity.

At day's end he was heading back to the hive, when, out of the corner of his eye, he saw a bee lying on the ground, obviously in trouble. Buzz dipped down to help when he saw it was Bert, pathetically trying to stand. A sudden wave of remorse and love melted his callousness as he watched his old friend struggling in vain. Bert was dying.

"I CAN'T TAKE ANY MORE!"

Buzz landed quickly and tried to comfort him, tears streaming down his cheeks. "I'm sorry, Bert. I'm so sorry," he sobbed. "Please forgive me."

"Nothing to bee sorry about, son," Bert whispered, clearly in pain. "You did what you had to do." Bert smiled at Buzz in a way that said, *All is forgiven.*

"How long have you been here, Bert?"

"Since about noon."

"Hang on," Buzz urged. "I'll bee right back with some nectar."

"No," said Bert.

"But, Bert, I can bring you food and..."

"No," Bert repeated calmly. "It's my time, Buzz. There's no sense prolonging it."

Overwhelmed, Buzz cried even harder and propped up the old bee's head as best he could. "Thank you so much for all you've given me, Bert. I'll always remember you."

Bert managed a faint smile and whispered, "Pass it on."

Buzz was surprised at the peace in Bert's face. "You haven't said a word about dying. Aren't you afraid?"

"Only when I forget who I really am," he whispered. The two bees gazed intently into each other's eyes and Bert continued

haltingly. "Buzz, I know your searching hasn't been easy...but if there's one thing...I want to leave you with...is that our existence here...isn't about our ideas of God...or religion...or the hereafter. It's about..."

"It's about..." Buzz interrupted as a rapt expression came over his face. "It's about right here, right now. Bee here now."

A look of immense contentment came over Bert's face. His mouth relaxed, his breathing grew shallow, his eyes closed, and Bert gently let go.

At that very moment, an exquisite nectar Buzz had never before tasted permeated his mouth and lingered as the reality of Bert's death overcame him. Buzz collapsed on the ground, lost in grief.

8

OVERWHELMED, Buzz passed most of the night in tears. Bert was the only bee he had ever loved, the only bee who had ever understood him, and now he was gone. Buzz already missed him terribly. He didn't know he could feel so alone, so sorrowful. It was the longest, saddest night of his life.

Buzz sobbed and sobbed until there were no more tears left. Still he stood there, silently mourning his old friend into the wee hours of the new day. Eventually a feeling of restlessness began to overcome him. What was he going to do now? He had to leave Bert sooner or later. He started for the hive, but it just didn't feel right, so he flew back to continue his vigil. He knew that it had been more than luck that Bert had appeared in his life when he did. The old-timer had given him so much, but now what was he supposed to do with it?

As dawn broke, he kept looking up at the peaks, lit in alpenglow, beckoning him. Buzz said a final farewell to his friend and teacher and was off as soon as the first rays of sunlight slipped over the horizon. He flew stiffly in the cold, but couldn't wait any longer. As he arrived at the tree line, Buzz stopped and looked up in awe. This truly was a miraculous place, and from now on he was going to experience more of it.

He fed on a few wildflowers to build his energy and then surveyed the range. It was still intimidating. But something else was bothering him; something didn't feel right. He tried to discern what it was, but with no luck. He was getting nervous, having second thoughts. *What am I doing up here?* he asked himself. *I must bee crazy. That wind is going to obliterate me on those cliffs.*

And then it hit him. WIND? THERE IS NO WIND! It was as though the air, in its silence, were beckoning him. His body shuddered with excitement as he bolted upward.

The first thousand feet went by like a jaunt to the meadow, before the realities of bee physiology caught up with Buzz. He hovered for a moment, regaining his energy, and surveyed the scene below. He had never been this high before. Down-valley the meadow looked like a tiny green patch on the valley floor. Above, another two thousand feet of sheer rock face seemed to mock his brazen intent. He continued climbing, this time at a more reasonable pace, now an upward spiraling, rather than direct ascent.

As he approached the halfway point, Buzz again began feeling drained. His wings, never before called on to do this kind of duty, ached in protest. He landed on a small rock outcropping to rest, and as he sat there, this tiny bee overseeing his magnificent valley, the reality of what he was doing finally hit him.

It was pristinely beautiful. The air was perfectly clear and crisp. The sky was a brilliant blue. To the left, a thin waterfall misted to the valley floor. A hundred shades of green reflected the morning sunshine. Beavers made the rounds of their ponds. Deer grazed in the lush meadow. Clouds drifted by, closer than ever before. Distant birdsong filled the air. Everything seemed alive!

"It is all truly perfect," Buzz said slowly to himself. "It all fits together; everything complements everything else. There are no mistakes. Good and bad are only within the minds of bees. It all just IS!" His body tingled as the memory of Bert's words crossed his mind.

HAPPINESS CANNOT BEE PURSUED;
IT MUST ENSUE.

A gust of wind brought him back to the moment. If he wanted to fly this pass today, he needed to get going, because a breeze was already kicking up. He lifted off and continued to climb—another two hundred,…four hundred,…six hundred feet. Yet the higher he got, the more the breeze became wind, and the tougher it was to maintain control.

He felt himself beeing buffeted about and missed smashing into an outcropping by a mere two feet. A downdraft erased a hundred feet of vertical progress in three seconds. Buzz sensed disaster and fought desperately to pull away from the rocks. His tiny wings were beating with everything he had, but he was running out of energy. He needed to land, and soon, but the air was far too unstable. Buzz was in big trouble, and he knew it.

Then came the gust he had been dreading. The last thing he remembered was frantically reversing as he was thrust at the side of the mountain, upside down, totally out of control.

9

BUZZ'S FIRST IMPRESSION when he came to was surprise. He looked around in disbelief. The wind had tossed him onto a narrow shelf 1,000 feet below the pass and it was raging now, stronger than ever. Buzz was groggy and weak and depleted, but he was alive. As he regained his senses, he slowly realized there was no way he could go any higher in this condition; in fact, there was no way he could go anywhere in this condition. He needed nectar, and badly.

He crawled back and forth, surveying his situation for any possibility of escape. Up, down, right, left—the only options were sheer rock face and roaring wind. Flying was out of the question. Slowly and reluctantly Buzz came to the realization that there was a good chance he was going to die up here.

Buzz felt numb. His ears began ringing. He couldn't believe it—he, Buzz Bee, was going to die. Not somebody else, not an old guy like Bert, but Buzz himself. Tomorrow he just wouldn't bee here anymore. He was so young. How could this bee happening to him? Here he was, following his dream, and now he was going to die for it. The world truly was an unfair place. A thousand thoughts raced uncontrolled through his terrified mind.

He tried to think of dying as going to sleep and just not waking up, but somehow it didn't seem to comfort him much. He wondered what it would bee like to starve to death, and how long it would take. He imagined what would happen to his body. It would decompose and dry out, a gust of wind would blow it off the edge, and it would bounce all the way down the rocks to the bottom. Then it would just lie there and rot. And no one would ever even know, or care, for that matter. It was all so terribly sad. Buzz began to lose control of his emotions—he cried, he quivered, he screamed, and he wailed, but his fear only grew worse. He thought of Bert and wondered what he would have to say.

THE ONLY WAY OUT IS IN.

Buzz sat there for the rest of the morning, growing increasingly drowsy, agonizing over the inevitable. At times he was overcome by fear and sadness. But then he'd think that he didn't want to

die this way and would manage to get hold of himself. For a while he'd bee able to contemplate his life and death rationally. But then his mind would get away from him, and the fear and sadness would again overwhelm him.

Increasingly Buzz noticed that he could hardly move and was having a difficult time thinking clearly. Everything was becoming fuzzy and dreamy. It was a pleasant respite from his earlier terror, and Buzz welcomed it. It really wasn't such a bad way to go after all.

Buzz was fading in and out of consciousness when, suddenly, out of the corner of his eye, he saw them. At first he thought he was hallucinating; he looked away, rubbed his eyes and then looked back again. They were still there—a small clump of three tiny wildflowers miraculously clinging to the cold, lifeless granite. He still couldn't quite believe it. He had spent the entire morning on this shelf. How could he possibly have overlooked these flowers? Was he dreaming?

Buzz dragged his depleted body over to the flowers and touched one. It was real! He rested for a moment at the stem, gathering his strength. Then with all his might, he struggled up, peered inside and saw, deep within, the tiny pistil, glistening with a thin coating of nectar. He squeezed inside and feasted. It was that same unique nectar he had tasted when Bert died! What was going on here? When he finished with the first flower, he moved on to the second, his energy slowly returning. By the time he was half done with it, Buzz was full and beginning to feel like his old self again.

He climbed down and looked back at the flowers, still not quite believing what had just happened. "What incredible luck," he said to himself. "How did those flowers get there? I couldn't possibly have overlooked them. And why do they taste exactly like the nectar I tasted when Bert died? In fact, why wasn't I killed when the wind slammed me against the rocks?" Exactly what was going on here this morning?

As he regained his strength, Buzz walked to the edge and looked down. A gust of wind blasted by, nearly taking him with it. He crouched, grasping a nub of granite until it passed. The wind was howling worse than ever, and Buzz knew there was no way he could take off until it died down. He found a sunny spot protected from the gale and relaxed. He knew that the wind usually died around sunset, and that at worst he'd probably just have to wait out the afternoon.

And so he sat, this bold little bee, overlooking his homeland. He knew now that he'd not only survive this ordeal, but that he was going to make it to the other side. Buzz felt incredibly alive; even more than he had as a youngster. He hummed his favorite tunes to pass the time. Every once in a while he'd return to the flowers for a sip of nectar and bee reminded all over again of Bert and his good fortune.

LIFE IS TOO IMPORTANT
TO BEE TAKEN SO SERIOUSLY.

Suddenly Buzz missed the old-timer terribly. Bert had been so kind and so helpful. Buzz had learned so much from him. He wished more than anything that Bert could bee here now.

The sun dropped lower and lower in the sky and the wind continued to howl. Still, Buzz remained confident that it would die once the sun set. But when the sun touched the horizon and then slowly sank out of sight without a hint of change in the wind, Buzz began to worry. He knew he had only an hour of light and warmth left to make it over the pass. The wind screamed worse than ever, and when the first star appeared, Buzz's spirits plummeted.

He was going to have to spend the night up here, exposed to this freezing wind. He didn't know if he could make it, but he had no choice but to try. As the hours passed and the evening chilled, Buzz grew colder and colder. He wedged himself into the most protected crevice he could find. Although the granite was dead cold, it was better than the wind. But soon he began shivering uncontrollably. He stepped back out onto the ledge to flap his wings and hop around, but it barely helped.

Buzz thought of his colony below, all snug and warm in the hive. It really wasn't so bad there after all. Why had he come up here? He realized how much he had in the colony and what a fool he had been to take it all for granted. He began to think that if the wind died down tomorrow, he would return and make a new life for himself. Just then the strongest gust of the night wailed through, shrieking Bert's admonition.

THERE'S NO TURNING BACK NOW;
YOU KNOW TOO MUCH.

Twice, in the wee hours of the morning, Buzz caught himself nodding off. It was the one thing he knew he couldn't let himself do, for if he didn't keep moving, he'd never wake up. He forced himself back out onto the shelf and hopped around. His feet were frozen, his body quaked, and his wings ached, but he forced himself to move. It was pure agony.

And so Buzz Bee spent the longest, most miserable night of his life, alternating between crevice and shelf, trying to keep warm, trying to stay alive.

Finally, after what seemed like an eternity, Buzz noticed a faint grayness in the eastern sky and then a lone bird singing in the distance. Bird song? An hour before, he couldn't have heard a bird singing if it had been right next to him. Through his frigid dullness he realized the wind had stopped; everything was perfectly still.

Dawn seemed to drag on forever. Buzz impatiently shivered through it, anticipation the only thing keeping him alive. Finally sunlight struck the peak and ever so slowly crept down the mountain. Buzz stiffly crawled to the highest point on his shelf and waited, quaking with cold. As the first rays of light hit him, tingles of delicious warmth surged through his body. Buzz had never realized sunlight could feel so good. That was another thing he'd never again take for granted.

Gradually his frozen body thawed and he began to feel like himself again. Buzz basked as never before, walking back and forth on the shelf, spreading his wings to the sun to catch every last photon of the wonderful warmth.

After taking a final sip of nectar, he was ready. He lifted off and, in the calmness of the morning air, spiraled up effortlessly. But as he approached the pass, he felt not excitement or anticipation, but a growing unease. And when he finally reached the top, he felt not elated but disappointed. The air remained still, and so he landed to collect his thoughts.

The new scene below surprised him, to say the least. What he beheld wasn't a mountain, glacier, desert, or ocean. It was a

valley very much like his own, forested with a meadow and a pond. Buzz suddenly and instinctively knew that life there would bee very much like the life he had left behind—same society, same problems, same him. He had come all this way—risked his life—and for what? For more of the same? What had he been expecting? He had never really thought it through.

His mind told him that since he had come this far, he should descend into this valley, explore it, and satisfy his curiosity. If he turned back now, he'd never know what it was like and it would bug him forever. But, knowing the difficulty of getting back home, he ran the risk of beeing stranded in this new land if he continued. Was he losing his courage? Would turning back now mean he had risked his life for nothing? It was all so confusing.

NO MATTER WHERE YOU GO,
THERE YOU ARE.

At the same time he had a growing sense that exploring this side wasn't the real reason he had flown up here. As Buzz mulled over his decision, he noticed a sense of relief and peace when he thought about returning home, and a sense of unease and disappointment when he thought about descending into this new valley. He finally came to the conclusion that whatever he had needed to learn from this journey, he had already learned by coming this far. This didn't make sense, but Buzz felt he must honor it.

THE MIND IS A WONDERFUL SERVANT
BUT A TERRIBLE MASTER.

Finally a gust of wind brought him back to the present. Without another thought, Buzz turned around, lifted off, and descended back into his valley.

10

DOWN AND DOWN he spiraled, the ease of the descent matching the difficulty of the ascent. Soon he was below the tree line and approaching the meadow. It was a beautiful, bright, clear morning, and the colony was just beginning to swing into full gear. The air was electric with the sound of foraging bees. It was a scene Buzz had resentfully witnessed a hundred times before, but now he gladly joined in. Buzz had never found such satisfaction from the simple act of foraging and, despite the fatigue from the night before, the day's work hardly bothered him. It felt so good to bee back home.

Very early the next morning, well before dawn, Boris stretched in his den. He too had been thinking about better alternatives and had hatched a scheme that seemed sure to work. He had noticed how slowly the bees moved in the early morning chill, and an idea had come to him. Why not attack their hive at the coldest time of day, when they were least expecting it and least able to respond? Boris emerged from his den and headed toward the hive. When it came into view, he stopped and assessed the situation. Not a bee in sight—perfect! He ambled the rest of the way to the tree, dug in his claws and began climbing. Still no bees—he could barely contain his delight. As he reached the hive, he drew back his arm and gave a mighty swat. The hive broke loose from the tree and crashed to the ground, crumpled and broken, honey oozing out onto the dirt.

The entire colony was awakened at once by the horrific jolt, taken totally by surprise. Three seconds later came the crushing blow of hitting the ground. Hundreds of bees were killed

instantly, while dozens of others found themselves stuck in honey, unable to move. Panic and chaos reigned. Those bees that weren't killed or incapacitated saw Boris stepping down from the tree and running toward them. Too stiff and groggy to mount a defense, most simply crawled away and let Boris have his reward. It didn't take long. Within ten minutes he had eaten every part of the hive that contained honey, and destroyed those parts that didn't. It was complete and utter disaster.

Buzz was one of the lucky ones. Surprisingly he remained calm.

PERFECTION ISN'T SOME STATE OF AFFAIRS; IT'S A STATE OF MIND.

He felt so helpless watching Boris destroy in ten minutes what had taken a lifetime to build. But he also remembered his plan and hoped it might give the colony a chance to start anew and ultimately bee better off. After licking his chops for what seemed an eternity, Boris gave a loud roar and ambled off.

The survivors assembled around the wreckage of the hive, extricating bees from the honey and comforting the injured, waiting for the sun to rise. Finally dawn came and the elders assessed the situation. "The queen is dead," said one somberly.

"What will we do?" asked a worker.

"We'll rebuild," said an elder. "There are enough of us left to start a new colony."

"But where?"

"We'll just have to find a new tree," came the reply. "And build further out on the limb."

"And post sentries overnight," another added.

Buzz didn't bother to rebut those comments. "I know a place where we can rebuild and bee safe from both Boris and thunderstorms." All eyes turned to him. "In the cliffs," he added. "Beyond the upper end of the meadow."

"Who ever heard of building a beehive in rocks?" Buster retorted. "Beehives are built in trees. Period."

"Hold on, hold on," the elder replied. "Yes, it's unorthodox, but that might not bee such a bad idea. Exactly what do you have in mind, Buzz?"

"Come on, I'll show you," said Buzz, lifting off.

The colony swarmed behind Buzz as he made his way to the cliffs. He stopped at the base, and the swarm covered a tree. Buzz pointed up to the cracks. "There, there, or there."

Accompanied by Buzz, the elders flew up to take a look. They hovered inside each, assessing its potential as their new home. Buzz pointed out the benefits and drawbacks of each crack—accessibility, exposure, size, anchor points, and so on. "Personally, I like the middle one the best," Buzz offered.

"Me too," agreed the elder, echoed by the rest. "It's settled then. We'll rebuild right here."

WE'RE ALL EACH OTHER'S STUDENTS AND TEACHERS.

With the colony's population reduced by nearly half and with fall just around the corner, there was no time to waste. Everyone began work in earnest that very morning and toiled nonstop until dark. Of necessity, this routine continued day after day, without break, until the new hive began to take shape and they again had some shelter and warmth. Like everyone else, Buzz found himself working harder than ever before. Rather than resenting it, he felt a new camaraderie with his fellow workers. Sure, they had a different approach to life than he did, but the truth bee told, he realized he had a lot more in common with them than not.

LIFE IS A JOURNEY FROM I TO WE.

Buzz did his share, but each day he made time to slip away to the spot by the stream where he had met Bert. Silently he sat there, eyes closed, lost in the gurgling of the stream. It was the antithesis of worker behavior, and Buzz often found his mind wandering incessantly. But he stuck with it, and over time he found that he enjoyed the calmness and rejuvenation and deepening sense of self it brought, and he was increasingly able to just...

BEE HERE NOW.

As the days passed, Buzz noticed himself feeling increasingly grateful—grateful for his life and for surviving and for home. It was so good to bee back home. How amazing that he existed in this beautiful valley, that he belonged to this successful colony. How amazing it was that he had eyes to see all this and a mind to comprehend and appreciate it. How amazing it was that these flowers were here, always ready to feed the colony. How amazing it was that they had a hive to protect them and produce new generations of bees. And how amazing it was that he had met Bert.

And so Buzz Bee resumed life as a worker—building the hive, feeding the larvae, keeping house, foraging, and storing honey and pollen. There was no longer any need to defend the colony against attack. The disdain Buzz used to feel toward his fellow workers became a thing of the past, replaced by a growing sense of fondness and compassion. The more secure he became in who he was, the less he was threatened by who they were. He saw beyond their fears and foibles, as he allowed himself his own, and he realized that they were all doing the best they could with what they had.

And so Buzz Bee came to understand they were all playing their perfect roles. Including him. Everything was the same; nothing had changed. Except him.

THE POWER OF THE MIND
LIES IN PERCEIVING DIFFERENCES;
THE POWER OF THE HEART
LIES IN PERCEIVING SIMILARITIES.